PLASTIC

LEVEL

WRITTEN BY CATRIN MORRIS
SERIES EDITOR: SORREL PITTS

PENGUIN BOOKS

UK | USA | Canada | Ireland | Australia
India | New Zealand | South Africa

Penguin Books is part of the Penguin Random House group of companies
whose addresses can be found at global.penguinrandomhouse.com.
www.penguin.co.uk www.puffin.co.uk www.ladybird.co.uk

First published 2019
001

Text written by Catrin Morris
Text copyright © Penguin Books Ltd, 2019

Printed in China

A CIP catalogue record for this book is available from the British Library

ISBN: 978–0–241–37522–8

All correspondence to
Penguin Books
Penguin Random House Children's Books
80 Strand, London WC2R 0RL

MIX
Paper from
responsible sources
FSC® C009967

Contents

New words

cup

environment

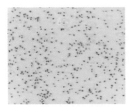
microbeads

nature

packaging

recycle (v)
recycling (n)

rubber

rubbish

single-use plastic

straw

Note about the book

Today, we use a lot of plastic. In the past, we did not have plastic. This is the story of how plastic was first made and what we use it for.

There is a lot of plastic in the world now. What do we do with it all? There are lots of good things about plastic, but there are lots of bad things about it, too. Countries, **companies*** and people are finding ways to stop **using** new plastic and to recycle more.

Before-reading questions

1   What did people use before plastic?

2   Think of the plastic things in your bag, bedroom or home. What are they?

3   Which of the things from question 2 do you really need?

4   What is good about plastic things?

5   What is bad about plastic things?

*Definitions of words in **bold** can be found in the glossary on page 63.

CHAPTER ONE

The story of plastic

There is a lot of plastic in the world today.
We **use** plastic bottles and plastic bags.
Plastic things can be big or small, **hard** or **soft**.

We eat food in plastic packaging, with plastic forks.

We drink from plastic cups, with plastic straws.

And we pay for things with plastic money.

At work and at school, we sit on plastic chairs at plastic tables.

Every day, we use plastic pens, computers and phones. Plastic is an important part of our world.

Before plastic, what did people make things with?

In the past, people took things from nature.

They used parts of animals to make things, and they used a lot of **plants** and trees.

Rubber comes from trees.
It is soft and **strong**.

Companies make lots of things from
rubber. They make **tyres**, clothes and toys.

Alexander Parkes made the first plastic, in England, in 1862.

Parkesine was a very hard plastic, but it could **break** or start fires.

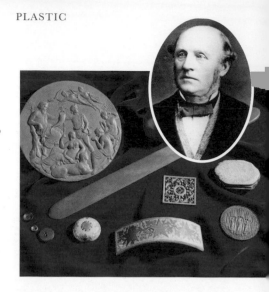

Then, American John Wesley Hyatt made games with celluloid in 1870.

A French company made clothes with rayon in 1891. Rayon was beautiful, but it was not strong.

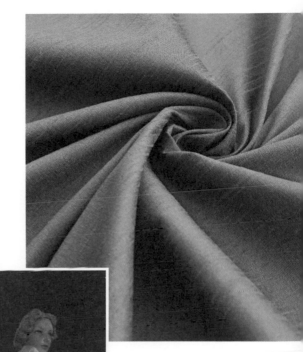

When people washed their rayon clothes, it sometimes made the clothes small.

Sometimes, the rayon clothes started fires.

Leo Baekeland made Bakelite in 1907.

Bakelite was **light** and strong.

People made clocks, toys, telephones and parts of cars with it. Bakelite was the start of today's plastics.

CHAPTER TWO

Plastics today

In the past, people did not often buy new things. They used old things again and again.

But, today, we buy a lot of new things. And many of those things are plastic.

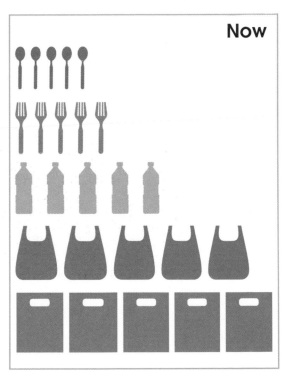

Today, we use different plastics for many different things.

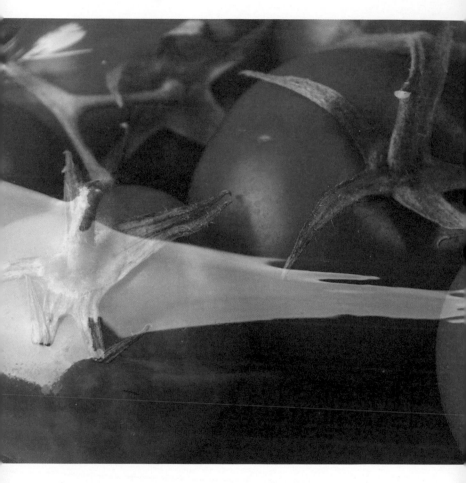

You find cellophane in food packaging. Cellophane is good because you can see the food inside it. The food stays clean and **dry**.

We usc a lot of polystyrene packaging and boxes because polystyrene is very light.

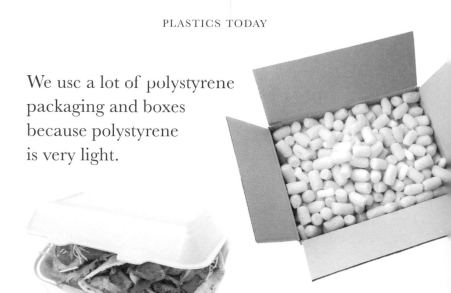

We make clothes from polyester. People can wash polyester clothes, and it does not make the clothes small.

We make plastic bottles and bags with polythene.

And we make lots of things for our homes and hospitals with PVC.

We use PET for drinks bottles. It is **clear** and strong.

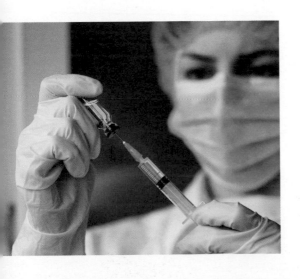

We use nylon for clothes, bags and things in the house, like curtains. It is very light and soft.

We use Teflon in the kitchen. It is strong, and it does not start fires.

You can find vinyl plastic in floors and on walls.

Vinyl was very important for the music world. **Records** were made from vinyl. People like playing records today, too.

CHAPTER THREE

Plastic at home

We like using plastic. Plastic things **last**.
They are strong, and they do not often break.

In the past, we made lots
of things from glass.
But glass breaks.

We made lots of things
from **wood**, too. But
wood does not last.

Plastic is **cheap**. In the past, new things were **expensive**.

Now you can buy plastic things. You do not need a lot of money.

We like plastic because it looks good.
Plastic can be different colours.

Some plastic is
clear. You can
see inside a
bottle, a box or
packaging.

In the past, we made things from animals, plants and trees. This was bad for the environment.

Now, we can make the same things from plastic.

We can buy food from
different countries now, too.

Food can travel. It lasts
because of plastic.

We do not have to go shopping every day.
Food lasts in the supermarket and at home.

We use a lot of plastic in hospitals, too.

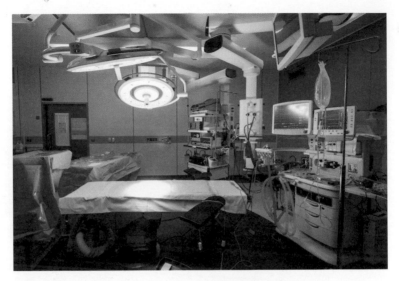

Plastic things can be very clean and dry. This is very important in hospitals.

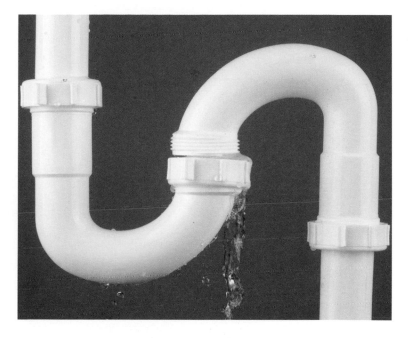

Plastic carries **energy** and water to our homes.

Because of plastic, we can be warm, and we can see at night. We can watch TV and cook our food. We can wash our bodies and our clothes.

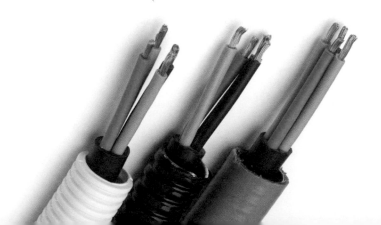

Today, we often travel by car, train, bus and plane.

There is very light plastic inside our cars, trains, buses and planes.

This light plastic **saves** energy. That is good for the environment and for us.

CHAPTER FOUR

Plastic and the environment

Plastic is not always bad.
We know why we make and
buy a lot of plastic things.

But what do we do with them next?

People buy 1,000,000 plastic bottles in the world every minute.

People also use 1,000,000 plastic bags in the world every minute.

Often, we use a plastic bag for only 25 minutes!

We often use plastic bottles, cups, straws, spoons and food packaging for only 5 minutes. Then we never use them again.

This is single-use plastic.

Where does our plastic rubbish go?
Plastic can stay in the environment
for hundreds of years.

Recycling is good. But we cannot always recycle plastic. Some things are not only plastic. They can be plastic and paper together.

Some of the plastic is dirty, or it is not dry.

A lot of plastic rubbish goes from our towns and our cities to rivers and the sea.

Every minute, rubbish from one lorry goes in the sea.

Animals in the sea eat this plastic rubbish.
They think it is food.

About 90% of
seabirds eat
plastic, too.
They give it to
their babies.

Every year, 100,000 sea animals die because of plastic in the sea.

Because we eat fish from the sea, we eat the plastic inside them, too. It is not good for us.

Microbeads are very small bits of plastic.

There are a lot of microbeads in these bottles.

We use these bottles in the bathroom, and the water goes to the sea. The microbeads stay there.

Now, there is a lot of plastic rubbish on **islands** in the sea.

People do not live on these islands, but the sea carries our rubbish to them.

Plastic rubbish makes new islands in the sea, too.

Small bits of plastic are in bottles of water.

We drink this water.
It is not good for us. It is not good for the environment.

CHAPTER FIVE

Recycling

We only recycle about 9% of plastic.

You cannot always recycle plastic. Recycling is not always cheap or easy. Some companies use single-use plastic for every cup of coffee.

Some companies use single-use plastic packaging for their food. This plastic is very cheap, and these companies make a lot of money.

Recycling does not use a lot of energy. You can recycle a lot of plastic at the same time. Recycling is good for the environment, and it is good for us.

You can make lots of new things from old plastic.

Ten plastic bottles can make a T-shirt.

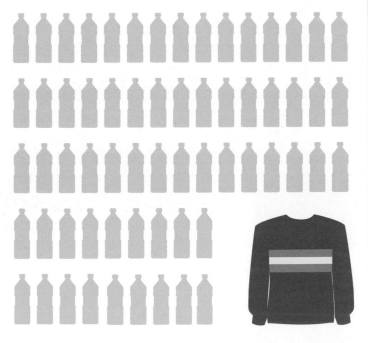

Sixty-three plastic bottles can make a sweater.

Which plastics can you recycle? People do not always know.

You can only recycle some plastics in some places.

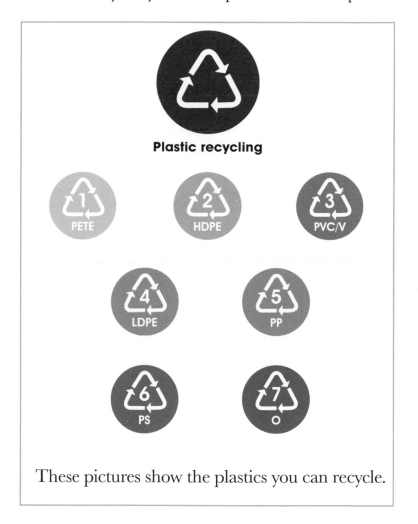

These pictures show the plastics you can recycle.

You cannot recycle dirty things with food or **chemicals** in them.

You have to clean them, and then you can recycle the plastic.

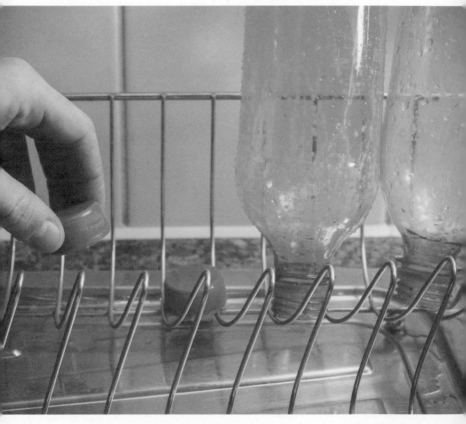

Today, machines can recycle a lot of different things.

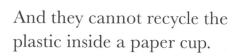

But they cannot recycle plastic and paper together.

And they cannot recycle the plastic inside a paper cup.

What can we do?

We can recycle more.
We can also stop using
single-use plastics.

We have to use
plastic things again.

And we can carry shopping bags with us.

What can we do with our rubbish?

We must take our rubbish with us from beaches and parks.

We have to think about the environment.

CHAPTER SIX

What next for plastic?

What are people, countries and companies
doing with their plastic rubbish?

People are doing lots of different things across
the world.

In Germany, Norway and Sweden, people recycle 90% of plastic bottles.

You pay a bit more for plastic bottles. You put your bottle in a machine, and you get some money back.

In some countries, shops do not give people any new plastic bags. Some examples of these countries are Bangladesh, Jamaica and Kenya.

In other countries, companies cannot make things with microbeads in them. Some examples are France, New Zealand and Sweden.

Some companies are making new cups. The cups are good for the environment because you can use them again. You can take them to coffee shops and save money on your coffee.

Some companies are making food boxes, plates, knives and forks from plants.

These things go back into the environment to grow new plants.

Now, people are finding new things in nature. These things can eat plastic.

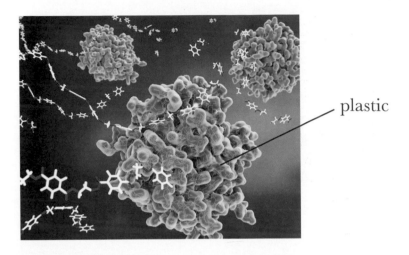

plastic

People are making new plastics, too. These plastics do not stay in the environment.

New machines can recycle lots of different plastics.

These machines put the same plastics together. Then they recycle them.

The United Nations and the European Union want to stop using as much plastic as they do now.

When	Who	What
2022	the United Nations	no single-use plastics
2030	the European Union	recycle all plastic packaging

We cannot live in a world with no plastic,
because we use plastic every day.

But we can save the world from the
plastic rubbish in our environment.

During-reading questions

Write the answers to these questions in your notebook.

CHAPTER ONE

1 What plastic things do we eat food with?
2 What plastic things do we sit on?
3 Where does rubber come from?
4 Why were rayon clothes bad?
5 What things were made from Bakelite?

CHAPTER TWO

1 Why do we use more plastic now than we did in the past?
2 What type of plastic do you find in food packaging?
3 In which two places might you find PVC?
4 Why is PET used to make drinks bottles?
5 What type of plastic are records made of?

CHAPTER THREE

1 Why do we make some things from plastic and not from glass or wood?
2 In which places are clean and dry plastic things very important?
3 What does plastic carry to our homes?

CHAPTER FOUR

1 What is single-use plastic?
2 Why can we not always recycle plastic?
3 Where does a lot of plastic rubbish go? Why is this bad?
4 What are microbeads?

1 How much plastic do we recycle?
2 What can you make with . . .
   a ten plastic bottles?   **b** sixty-three plastic bottles?
3 What can we do to stop plastic rubbish?

1 Which countries are recycling 90% of plastic bottles?
2 In which countries do shops not give people new plastic bags?
3 Which countries do not make new things with plastic microbeads?

After-reading questions

1 What do we make from rubber?
2 Who made the first plastic? When and where?
3 Why do we use a lot of plastic?
4 What is bad about plastic?
5 What do you do with your plastic rubbish?

Exercises

1 **Write the correct prepositions in your notebook.**

in	from	at	of	on	with

1   We eat food ....*in*.......... plastic packaging, with plastic forks.
2   We drink .... plastic cups, with plastic straws.
3   And we pay for things .... plastic money.
4   At work and at school, we sit .... plastic chairs ....
     plastic tables.
5   Plastic is an important part .... our world.

CHAPTERS ONE AND TWO

2 **Write the opposite of these words in your notebook.**
1   big ....*small*......
2   hard
3   old
4   dirty

CHAPTER THREE

3 **Order the words to make sentences in your notebook.**
1   plastic like using We . ...*We like using plastic*..........
2   Wood last not does .
3   colours be Plastic different can .
4   because plastic Food of lasts .
5   energy light saves This plastic .

4 Match the pictures to the words. Write the answers in your notebook.

Example: 1 – b

1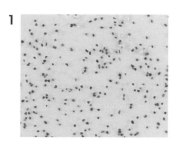

2

3

4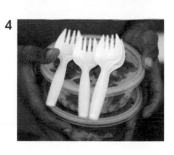

5

6

a environment   **b** microbeads

c cups   **d** recycling

e rubbish   **f** packaging

CHAPTER FOUR

5 **Write the correct adverbs of frequency in your notebook.**

1   We **never /** *often* use plastic bottles, cups, straws, spoons and food packaging for only five minutes.

2   Then we **always / never** use them again. This is single-use plastic.

3   We cannot **always / sometimes** recycle plastic.

4   **Always / Sometimes** the plastic is dirty, or it is not dry.

5   Animals in the sea **often / never** eat this plastic rubbish.

CHAPTER FIVE

6 **Are these sentences** *true* **or** *false*? **Write the answers in your notebook.**

1   Recycling is always easy. ....*false*........

2   Recycling is good for the environment.

3   You cannot make new things from old plastic.

4   You cannot recycle some plastics in some places.

5   You do not have to clean dirty plastic before you recycle it.

6   Machines cannot recycle paper and plastic together.

CHAPTERS FIVE AND SIX

7 **Complete these sentences in your notebook, using** *Some, any* **or** *a lot of.*

1   ....*Some*.......... companies use single-use plastic for every cup of coffee.

2   Single-use plastic is very cheap, and the companies make .... money.

3   Recycling does not use .... energy.

4   We can make .... new things from old plastic.

5   Some countries do not give people .... new plastic bags.

CHAPTER SIX

8 **Read the answers, and write the correct question words in your notebook.**

1 ......*What*......... are people, countries and companies doing with their plastic rubbish?
People are doing lots of different things across the world.

2 .... countries recycle 90% of plastic bottles?
Germany, Norway and Sweden.

3 .... would the United Nations like no single-use plastics?
In 2022.

4 .... would like to recycle all plastic packaging?
The European Union.

5 .... can we not live in a world with no plastic?
Because we use plastic every day.

9 **Correct these sentences in your notebook.**

1 You cannot recycle any plastic bottles in Sweden.
You can recycle plastic bottles in Sweden.

2 You do not have to pay more for plastic bottles in Sweden.

3 You put your bottle in a machine, and you cannot get any money back.

4 Shops in Bangladesh give people new plastic bags.

5 In France, companies can make new things with plastic microbeads in them.

Project work

1 Ask your friends these questions.
   - What do you do with your plastic rubbish?
   - Which single-use plastics do you use?
   - Do you use things with microbeads?
   - Are you good at recycling?

2 Write a newspaper report about plastic rubbish in your town or country. In your report, say:
   - where the rubbish is
   - how it got there
   - why it is bad for the environment
   - what people are doing about it.

3 Make a school recycling poster. On your poster, say:
   - what you can recycle
   - where you can recycle things
   - how you can use things again.

An answer key for all questions and exercises can be found at **www.penguinreaders.co.uk**

Glossary

break (v) to make something go into small parts by hitting it

cheap (adj) If something is *cheap*, you do not need a lot of money to pay for it.

chemical (n) A *chemical* is a special liquid. Scientists make and use chemicals. They are not from nature.

clear (adj) easy to see through

company (n) A *company* makes and sells things. People work for a *company*.

dry (adj) If something is *dry*, it has no water on it.

energy (n) *Energy* makes machines work.

expensive (adj) If something is *expensive*, you need a lot of money to pay for it.

hard (adj) like rock; not moving in when you put your finger on it

island (n) a country, or a part of a country, with water on every side of it

last (v) If something *lasts*, it stays in the world for a long time.

light (adj) not heavy; easy to move

plant (n) a living thing, like a tree. It grows in the ground.

record (n) A *record* plays music with a special machine. It is made from plastic and is flat, round and black.

save (v) to not use as much of something as you used before; to stop bad things happening to something or someone

soft (adj) not *hard*; moving in when you put your finger on it

strong (adj) not breaking easily

tyre (n) a thick, round piece of rubber. It goes on the wheel of a car.

use (v) to do something with a thing so that you can do a job

wood (n) the *hard* thing that comes from the big, long part of a tree. People often make tables from *wood*.

14.1.20

St. Julians

Penguin Readers

Visit www.penguinreaders.co.uk
for FREE Penguin Readers resources.

Photo credits

Cover (plastic bottles) © venusvi/shutterstock.com; pages 4, 8 and 59 (cup and straw) © 5 second Studio/Shutterstock.com; pages 4 and 59 (environment) iStock.com/Kalistratova; pages 4, 37 and 59 (microbeads) © KYTan /Shutterstock.com; pages 4 and 10 (nature) © istock.com/Anrodphoto; pages 4, 8 and 59 (packaging) © Ingetje Tadros/Getty Images; pages 4 and 59 (recycle/recycling) iStock.com/Rawpixel; pages 4 and 11 (rubber tyres) © iStock.com/deepblue4you; pages 4, 29 and 59 (rubbish) © iStock.com/vchal; pages 4 and 31 (single-use plastic) © iStock.com/csfotoimages; pages 6–7 (the story of plastic) © iStock.com/curtoicurto; page 8 (credit card) © leolintang/shutterstock.com; page 9 (plastic chairs) © pramot/shutterstock.com; page 9 (plastic pens) © Rugged Studio/Shutterstock.com; page 10 (elephant) © iStock.com/Hirkophoto; page 11 (man and tree) © iStock.com/Gastuner19; page 11 (duck) © Marques/shutterstock.com; page 12 (Alexander Parkes) copyright ©Science & Society Picture Library / Getty Images; page 12 (Parkesine) copyright ©Science & Society Picture Library / Getty Images; page 12 (John Wesley Hyatt) copyright ©Granger Historical Picture Archive / Alamy Stock Photo; page 12 (celluloid game) copyright ©Steve Hamblin / Alamy Stock Photo; page 13 (green rayon) © istock.com/Radionphoto; page 13 (clothes on fire) copyright ©John Chillingworth/PicturePost/Getty Images; page 14 (Bakelite clock) DutchScenery /Shutterstock.com; page 14 (Bakelite cat) copyright ©DE AGOSTINI PICTURE LIBRARY / Getty Images; page 14 (Bakelite phone) © Billion Photos/shutterstock.com; page 16 (tomatoes) dedmityay/123rf.com; page 17 (polystyrene food container) © neil langan/Shutterstock.com; page 17 (polystyrene packaging) © iStock.com/deepblue4you; page 17 (clothes) © Tim Bird/Shutterstock.com; page 18 (bottles on conveyor belt) © Alba_alioth/Shutterstock.com; page 18 (syringe and doctor) © alexkich/Shutterstock.com; pages 18–19 (line of bottles) © iStock.com/scisettialfio; page 19 (curtains) © iStock.com/runna10; page 19 (Teflon™ pan) © Gregory Gerber/Shutterstock.com; page 20 (vinyl flooring) © U.J. Alexander/Shutterstock.com; page 20 (wall) © iStock.com/chulii; page 20 (record player) © iStock.com/lisegagne; page 21 (broken glass) © Jens_Lambert_Photography; page 21 (broken bench) © MrGoSlow/Shutterstock.com; pages 22–23 (coloured bottles) © Denis Tabler/Shutterstock.com; page 22 (clock) © Istomina Olena/Shutterstock.com; page 22 (teapot and cups) © Daniil Yanopulo/shutterstock.com; page 22 (beads) © Alena Ozerova/Shutterstock.com; page 22 (coloured cups) © nuttakit/Shutterstock.com; page 23 (clear containers with fruit on shelf) © littlenySTOCK/Shutterstock.com; page 24 (felled trees) © Kaichankava Larysa/Shutterstock.com; page 24 (coat) © iStock.com/robertprzybysz; page 24 (handbag) © Danny Iacob/Shutterstock.com; page 25 (coffee) © iStock.com/kcline; page 25 (shelves in supermarket) © Salvador Aznar/Shutterstock.com; page 26 (operating theatre) © iStock.com/JohnnyGreig; page 26 (surgeon and gloves) © iStock.com/Steve Debenport; page 27 (plastic pipe) © iStock.com/Scukrov; page 27 (cables) © iStock.com/freeman98589; page 28 (tube train) © iStock.com/fotoVoyager; page 28 (inside bus) © Shuang Li/shutterstock; page 28 (inside plane) © Filipe Frazao/Shutterstock.com; page 30 (holding bottle) © Daniel Jedzura/Shutterstock.com; page 30 (holding bags) © iStock.com/IpekMorel; page 32 (beach rubbish) © iStock.com/FabioFilzi; page 33 (mixed food and cup) © wk1003mike/Shutterstock.com; page 33 (empty food container) © natrot/Shutterstock.com; page 34 (rubbish on lake) © iStock.com/Picturesd; page 35 (turtle and bag) © Rich Carey/Shutterstock.com; page 35 (penguin feeding chicks) © Photodynamic/Shutterstock.com; page 36 (turtle with rubbish on its head) © Kwangmoozaa/Shutterstock.com; pages 36–37 (underwater) © vovan/Shutterstock.com; page 37 (bottles with microbeads) © KYTan/Shutterstock.com; page 38 (island in sea) © istock.com/Utopia_88; pages 38–39 (bottles in dirty water) © istock.com/luoman; page 39 (pouring water) © Mariyana M/Shutterstock.com; page 40 (coffee cup) © istock.com/cveltri; page 40 (microwave meal) © istock.com/mg7; page 44 (dirty plastic cup) © Picsfive/Shutterstock.com; page 44 (washing bottles) © Lolostock/Shutterstock.com; page 45 (man at recycling machine) copyright © Ulrich Baumgarten/Getty Images; page 45 (sandwich box) © CHALN_CHAI/Shutterstock.com; page 45 (paper cup) © mnun/Shutterstock.com; page 46 (drinking bottle) © istock.com/JenniferPhotographyImaging; page 46 (packed lunch) © Katarzyna Białasiewicz/123rf.com; page 46 (net bag) © RossHelen/Shutterstock.com; page 47 (clearing beach) © iStock.com/vgajic; page 48 (sorting recycling) © junpinzon/Shutterstock.com; page 49 (bottle machine) copyright ©Walter G Allgower/Imagebroker/REX/Shutterstock; page 51 (ecoffee cup) Courtesy of ecoffeecup.eco; page 51 (food boxes) Courtesy of Vegware vegware.co.uk; page 52 (things eating plastic) © Juan Gaertner/shutterstock.com; page 52 (compostable plastic) copyright ©Angela Hampton Picture Library / Alamy Stock Photo; page 53 (rubbish on machine) copyright ©Hermann Bredehorst / Polaris / eyevine; page 55 (fish made of rubbish) © Nagy-Bagoly Arpad/Shutterstock.com; page 62 (diver with basket of plastic) ©DPA DEUTSCHE PRESS-AGENTUR/DPA/PA Images